IN THE HOUSE
Turn

MW01110303

Contents

Introduction	3
How to Use This Journal	4
Action Step Preview	5
Get Your Ears Pierced (Action Step 1)	6
The Pierced Ears Prayer	7
Catch the Rave (Action Step 2)	8
Cross the Lines (Action Step 3)	9
Electrify a Friend (Action Step 4)	11
Take Out the Trash (Action Step 5)	12
Warm-up Days	13
Everybody Matters (Theme 1)	15
Days 1–6	17
You Can Bring Your Friends (Theme 2)	23
Days 7–13	25
It's Okay to Be Me (Theme 3)	31
Days 14–20	33
We Help Each Other Be All We Can Be (Theme 4)	39
A Few Good Words	40
Days 21–27	44
People Are Real (Theme 5)	50
Days 28–34	53
We Make a Difference (Theme 6)	59
Days 35–41	61
God Shows Up (Theme 7)	67
Days 42–46	69
The Future Looks Bright (Theme 8)	73
Days 47–50	74
Last Words	79

Written by Randy Petersen, Jim Hancock, and Mitch Vander Vorst

Editor: Mitch Vander Vorst
Cover Design: Tony Laidig
Cover Illustration: Bethany Hissong
Text Design: Blum Graphic Design

Copyright © 1996 The Chapel of The Air Ministries, Inc.
Published by The Chapel Ministries
Dr. David R. Mains, Director

The Chapel Ministries is a nonprofit, nondenominational, international Christian outreach dedicated to helping God's church grow spiritually and numerically by revitalizing its members, whether they be gathered or scattered, to be a force for kingdom purposes worldwide. To support this goal, The Chapel Ministries provides print and media resources including the annual 50-Day Spiritual Adventure and 4-Week Worship Celebration, the daily half-hour television program "You Need to Know," and seasonal radio programming. Year-round Bible study guides are offered through a Joint Ministry Venture with Scripture Union U.S.A., to encourage the healthy spiritual habits of daily Scripture reading and prayer.

Printed in the United States of America.

ISBN 1-57849-001-4

we all know people who liven up the room when they walk in. When they're in the house the party is really going. Everyone laughs and talks and has a good time. Jokes fly left and right. Everybody wants such people around.

Well, *Ladies and gentlemen, in the house tonight is a special guest. Please give it up for . . . <u>Jesus Christ!</u>*

We don't hear that very often in our churches, but why not? We believe Jesus is present with us as we meet together. He is *in the house*—hey, it's his house!

What would happen if he really did take the stage? Oh, we would sing his praises and he'd probably give the sermon, but then what? Would we ever muster up the guts to say, *How are we doing, Lord? Are we becoming the church you want us to be?*

And if we asked, how would Jesus answer?

Maybe he'd say, *Yes, you're doing fine.* But chances are he would challenge us—at least a little.

Then, the Lord might look tenderly across our faces, caressing our souls. *I love you,* he'd say. *Words can't express how much I love you. I'm not trying to make you feel guilty; I'm trying to help you do better. I want to help you be strong and caring and real. Will you stop resisting me and let that happen?*

Do you ever want your youth group or even your church to be more than it is? Do you ever feel like you don't belong? Or are you embarrassed or afraid to bring your friends to youth group? Is everybody the same? Are people helping to bring out the best in you? Are people real instead of hypocrites? Does your church make a difference in the world?

When Jesus is in the house, things change. The whole house changes. When you realize that Jesus is present in your church, even in your youth group, it should change the way you do business.

He wants your church, your youth group, you, to be so much more. Can we start letting him transform us? During the next 50 days you'll be beginning that transformation.

What happens when Jesus is in the house? That's what this Adventure is all about. When Jesus is in the house . . .

Theme 1: Everybody matters.
Theme 2: You can bring your friends.
Theme 3: It's okay to be me.
Theme 4: We help each other be all we can be.
Theme 5: People are real.
Theme 6: We make a difference.
Theme 7: God shows up.
Theme 8: The future looks bright.

And the five action steps will be a way for <u>you</u> to help turn your youth group or church inside out and make it a place where Jesus is in the house.

how to use this Journal

• <u>Pray</u> that God will help you in a special way during the next 50 days. Ask him what changes he'd like to see in your life through this Adventure.

• <u>Commit</u> yourself to being serious about this Adventure. If you give it some time and attention, there's a great payoff. Check it out for a few days, and then try to make a solid commitment before the first week is over.

• <u>Honesty</u> is the best policy. Be brutally honest with yourself, and with God, as you answer the questions in this journal. You can always use code words if you're afraid of someone snooping.

• <u>Relax.</u> If you miss a day, don't drive yourself crazy trying to make up for lost time. Just resume the journal on the current day. Later you can go back and see what you missed.

• <u>Connect</u> with others. Try doing this Adventure with a few friends, your family, or your youth group. You can hold each other accountable and provide new ideas for each other.

• <u>Prepare</u> yourself by glancing through the journal now, especially the introductory material on pages 3–12. See what's coming up. During the Adventure you'll take five action steps. Some may be fairly basic and familiar; others involve more preparation. But don't worry! The Looking Back/Moving Forward pages before each Sunday will help you keep on track. The warm-up days, Friday and Saturday before Day 1 (pp. 13–14), are optional, but they can get you off to a good start.

The top of each page in this journal has a place for the date. Take a moment now to locate a calendar. Find the Sunday you plan to begin the Adventure. Write that date in the blank on Sunday, Day 1. Then write the dates, in order, on all the pages that follow.

• <u>Expect</u> to grow. Great things can happen to you as you do this Adventure. God moves in mighty ways when his people let the Holy Spirit work through them. He can make a big difference in your life too.

• <u>Ask</u> questions. Don't expect to know or learn everything on your own. There may be some things that you just don't get. At the end of each day's reading is a space to write down your unanswered questions—what you don't know, don't understand, or just don't get. Don't write these down and forget about them. Try to get them answered—do some research on your own, ask someone who might be able to help, or talk about these questions in your youth group or at church.

• <u>Spend</u> some extra time. Each week read a chapter in Dan Lupton's book, <u>I Like Church, But . . .</u> This book will go into detail on the themes and action steps you will be tackling every day. (Read the introduction before Day 1.) Contact your church, local Christian bookstore, or The Chapel Ministries (1-800-224-2735 in the U.S., or 1-800-461-4114 in Canada) to order your copy.

action step preview

As you get farther into the Adventure, you can refer back to this list for a brief review of the action steps and how often you're to do each one. (For a more complete description of the action steps, see pp. 6–12.) Don't worry about keeping everything in your head. This journal will remind you of all your assignments on the Looking Back/Moving Forward pages.

every day

• <u>Read</u> the assigned Scripture passages and answer the questions in the journal.

• <u>Pray</u> the Pierced Ears Prayer using the words on page 7 as a guide (Action Step 1, p. 6).

• <u>Catch the rave</u> and write down something good about your youth group or church on pages 40–41 (Action Step 2, p. 8).

every week

• <u>Read</u> the appropriate chapter in Dan Lupton's book I Like Church, But ...

• <u>Rave</u> to a friend about your youth group or church (Action Step 2, p. 8).

twice

• <u>Cross</u> the lines and get together with someone outside your normal circle of friends (Action Step 3, p. 9).

once

• <u>Catch the rave</u> and invite someone to church (Action Step 2, p. 8).

• <u>Electrify a friend</u> and help bring out his or her potential (Action Step 4, p. 11).

• <u>Take out the trash</u> in your life (Action Step 5, p. 12).

action Step 1

get your ears pierced

every day

Superman is out for a stroll with Lois and he suddenly stops.

What's wrong, Supe? Lois asks tenderly. *That suit riding up again?*

No, says the superhero. *I hear something. A cry for help.*

Sure enough, seven states away, some little boy is trapped in a kryptonite mine. With his superpowers, our hero could hear that distant call as clearly as if it were on MCI.

Now consider a less-than-super character, Joe. He's out for a stroll with his girlfriend, uh, Jo.

So how are you, Jo? he asks ('cause girls dig sensitive guys).

Kind of depressed, Joe, she answers. *How are you?*

Couldn't be better, Joe crows. *I got this awesome new Sega game!* He goes on for fifteen minutes talking about all the mutants he wailed on. Meanwhile, Jo is still kind of depressed. Probably more depressed.

Earth to Joe! Earth to Joe! You just heard a cry for help without realizing it. The girl beside you desperately needs a reason to live, but you're blathering about getting to the third bonus round.

Joe needs to get his ears pierced. No, not at the Piercing Pagoda at the mall. Rather, a simple message needs to pierce through all the trivia cluttering his brain: GIRLFRIEND DEPRESSED! SEND HELP NOW!

We all have times when we're just not picking up the SOS signals around us. There's too much static— games and grades, dates and data, zingers and zits. We need something to pierce through all of the unimportant stuff so we can hear when our friends need help—really hear.

Imagine how cool it could be to have a bunch of Christians listening to one another, tuning in to each person's needs. That's the kind of group you'd want to be a part of, right? Well, you can start the process by asking Jesus to pierce <u>your</u> ears, to penetrate all the junk in your life and help you listen. And he can do it. He is a superhero with exceptional powers of hearing—and he can share those powers with you.

Make it so:

Pray the Pierced Ears Prayer every day of the Adventure. Of course, before you pray it, you need to recall some of the messages you've been hearing—the needs of those around you. That's the part of the prayer you need to fill in every day. This might be tough at first, but soon you'll become a regular satellite dish, tuning in to all sorts of signals.

Make this prayer your own. Change the words if you feel like it. And feel free to pray it several times a day.

the pierced ears prayer

Lord,

i WAnt To LOVe pEoPlE THE wAY YOU do,

But SoMEtiMeS iT's liKE i Don't EVEN heAr WhaT ThEy'RE saYiNg.

PlEAsE TeACh mE tO liSTen wItH Your ears.

i PRAy For: _____.

a need you've heard recently

lORd, hElP me TO bE AN EvEn BeTtER LIStEneR,

AND ShOw Me if i cAn do anyThiNG To HeLP.

amEn.

action step 2

Catch the rave every day

Hey, man! Party tonight. Jackie's place. Pass it on.

I thought it was at Wilson's.

They moved it. Jackie has the coolest house. It's gonna be jumpin'!

Hey! Party tonight. You coming?

By word of mouth the excitement builds. And chances are, the party will be great, simply because everyone expects it to be. Even before people show up, they're psyched for a good time.

Hey! Church. Sunday morning. Pass it on.

Where?

The big stone building on the corner. They say God's gonna show up. It'll be awesome!

Hey! Church. Sunday morning. You coming?

Church, and even your youth group activities can become like the food in your school cafeteria. Everyone loves to complain about it, but they'll still steal it off your tray. Even if by some miracle the food is actually pretty good one day, no one will be caught dead saying anything good about it. Complaining is just the cool thing to do.

If people think church and youth group meetings are boring and irrelevant, you may be contributing to that impression. How? By saying things like, *My parents are making me do church this weekend.* Or by keeping silent about the good things that happen in your youth group.

Break the silence! Stand up against this self-censorship by daring to say good things about your church or youth group. Turn your rips into raves! (No one's saying to make things up. We're not talking about pure propaganda and PR. We're talking about the genuinely good things about your church and youth group.)

Make it so:

Every day of the Adventure, write down something good about your church or youth group. (Use the Few Good Words chart on pp. 40–41.) Good things might include the support you feel from your friends, the good teaching you get, or specific examples of good times you've had. It could even be the great pizza party you had the other night.

Then, once a week, rave about your church or youth group to someone else. (A couple of times you could rave to someone else who's in your church or youth group, but try to include several outsiders also.)

Finally, before this Adventure is over, invite somebody to a church service or youth group meeting.

action Step 3

Cross the lines twice

Here's an idea for you, something that will make things easier for everyone at your school. Paint lines on the floors of the hallways. Each lane will be designated for a certain group. The smart kids will get the lane closest to the classrooms and the jocks will get the outside passing lane. Then the musicians, freaks, social animals, and rich kids each get their own lanes. Each person will know where he or she belongs. Stay within the lines and everyone will know who you are; you'll be with others who are just like you. It's amazing your school hasn't already thought of this!

You could have designated areas for each group to hang out in. Brains can have the library. Jocks, the gym. Rich kids, the parking lot. And all those other people can have the place in the back with all the cigarette butts.

Chances are, you already have some of these divisions at school. No lines on the floor, but people tend to hang with their own—don't they?

The fact is, these lines exist everywhere. The lines aren't painted on the ground—they don't have to be. Some schools have pretty sharp racial divisions. Or the rich students never talk to the poor students, or the brains stay away from those who aren't doing so hot in school. And the lines last after that final bell rings and everyone goes home.

One of the great things about Jesus is that he crosses the lines (and he uses a real cross). You don't have to be smart, rich, or athletic to be with Jesus. Humility is the key. He accepts all who come to him.

Sometimes we Christians find it easy to hang around with the other Christians and ignore everyone else. Or we find our particular niche of society and stay inside those lines. Jesus challenges us to cross the lines with him. In fact, he drags us across them.

Make it so:

Make friends with two new people during this Adventure. Follow these steps.

Step 1. Check out your group. On a piece of paper list the names of the people you generally hang with. Next to their name write what *group* they would belong to (jocks, brains, partiers, youth groupies, etc.). What is similar about most of the people you listed? Are they all white or black or Hispanic? Are they all rich or poor? Are they all popular or not? Are they all Christians?

And what about your not-so-close friends—your acquaintances and the people you talk to occasionally or say *hi* to as you pass by?

When you've analyzed your list of names, take a look at your chart and see what's missing. Where are the holes? Who is <u>not</u> represented in your life? Spend some time thinking about this. Is God telling you anything about a line you need to cross?

(continued on p. 10)

Cross The Lines

(continued from p. 9)

Step 2. Choose one person from a group other than your usual one. In the next step, you'll try to get to know this person better. Ask God to help you find a person who could use a friend.

Step 3. Try to get to know the person you've selected. Sit with him or her in the cafeteria or library, or go out for Cokes and fries. Ask questions that will help you get to know each other. (For a little help with this part, we've included some questions at the bottom of the page.)

(A few cautions: First, your aim in this exercise is not to win this person to the Lord, but merely to get to know each other. Don't be pushy about your faith. Second, be extremely careful about guy-girl relationships. If you choose to make friends with someone of the opposite sex, make it clear that it's not a *date,* but just a friendly get-together. Third, if the person doesn't want to talk with you, don't force the issue. Choose someone else.)

Step 4. The second friend we want you to make is someone in your own church. You see, there are lines of division within the church too, and one of the thickest is age. Chances are, you don't talk much with people older than you in your church.

So, repeat steps 2 and 3 with someone who's quite a bit older than you are. First, choose someone to befriend (perhaps with your parent's advice). Consider someone who interests you (someone with a job you're interested in, a war veteran, an ex-hippie, etc.) Then talk with that person at church. You might just chat for a while in between services or meet with the person in the church library. Just get to know each other a little bit.

This action step is completed when you've had a meaningful conversation (which might lead to a good friendship) with two people: (1) Someone from another group at school or in your youth group or your community; and (2) Someone older than you in your church.

Tips for Crossing the Lines

Here are some questions that may help you get to know each other.

1. What's your family like? Do you have brothers or sisters?
2. What's your favorite and least favorite school subject?
3. What TV shows do you watch? What about music, movies, video games, sports?
4. What do you like to do on weekends?
5. What do you like most about being your age? What frustrates you most about your age?
6. What are your plans for the future?
7. If you could become anyone else in the world for a day, who would it be?
8. If you could ask God a question right now, and you knew he'd answer you, what would you ask?

Of course, you're not interviewing the person for *60 Minutes.* You're just starting a conversation. Relax. Be a friend.

action Step 4

electrify a friend

once

Unsolved mystery. Two boom boxes—identical. One is blasting tunes at high volume; the other's completely silent. Hmmm. Some sinister plot to wreck the entertainment industry as we know it? Or maybe one's just missing batteries.

With batteries, the first box has the power to boom. Without that electricity, the second one is just an odd piece of post-modern sculpture.

People are like that, too. Odd pieces of postmodern sculpture? Well, perhaps, but what we're saying here is that they need power, that they need a kind of electricity to help them do what they were created to do.

You can *electrify* your friends. (Not elect*rocute* them.) How? By complimenting them on the things they do well. By helping them identify their areas of skill. By giving them opportunities to use their skills. By encouraging them along the way.

In these ways, you can help empower them to be all they can be, and you can energize them to be all God wants them to be. Think of yourself as the Energizer Bunny. But you don't need the drum and rabbit ears, all right?

Make it so:

This action step has three parts.

Part 1: Make the connection. Spend a week or two looking around you for people with hidden talents. Look for people with *silent* skills that are being overlooked by almost everyone else. Then pray and ask God to lead you to invest your effort in someone.

Once God has directed you, talk to the person. Let him or her know that you have noticed this hidden ability. Don't be surprised if the person is bashful. Be ready to give specific examples of when and how you have observed the person in action:

I think you're a really caring person. Last week you went out of your way to make that new kid feel comfortable.

That article you wrote for the church newsletter was fun to read. I'd love to see more of your writing.

The other kids look up to you a lot. Just today you said something in youth group, and it was like everyone respected your opinion. You could be a good leader.

Part 2: Listen for feedback. Ask the person about his or her dreams and ideas. Ask, don't tell. This is not your project—it's that person's life. You are offering your services to help that person make some of his or her dreams real for the glory of God.

Part 3: Turn on the music. See if you can help this person find good ways to use his or her abilities. Consider specific tasks in your church, youth group, or community that this person might be good at. In a way, you need to become an *agent* for this person, looking for opportunities for your *client.* Don't just make suggestions. Go ahead and make calls and do research for your *client.*

Encouragement. Advice. Research. Publicity. You can *electrify* your friend in all these ways, and many more.

action step 5

take out the trash

once

What's your room like? Completely anal retentive—a place for everything and everything in its place? The pleasant lived-in look? The who-knows-what room with clothes over chairs and piles all over? Or the condemned-by-the-board-of-health room?

It's amazing how quickly a lived-in look turns into an archaeological excavation with *treasures* like Friday night's sweater, Wednesday's late-night snack, and old Star Wars figures you can't bear to throw away.

What's your life like? Neat or not? How is your relationship with God? Is it as messy as your room? How would you begin to clean it up? Well, you need to start by *taking out the trash,* but what *trash* are we talking about? What trashes your relationship with God? Here are some possibilities:

First, look at the objects in your life that might keep you from following God. That swimsuit calendar above your bed is probably not helping you think pure thoughts. That CD by Christian Death is probably not bolstering your spiritual life.

But don't stop with the sexy and satanic. What objects are becoming idols for you? What can't you stop thinking about? Maybe you're past baseball cards and Barbie dolls, but your CD collection, your sports or fashion magazines, and your car could all become obsessions for you, distracting you from God.

Second, look at the relationships that might be hurting your relationship with God. Bad things can mess up good relationships. Does lust threaten to destroy an otherwise great romance? Do jealousy and anger weaken your interactions with classmates?

Finally, look at your own heart. Is pride or greed taking you away from God?

Here's the problem with having a sloppy room. The lived-in look is fine, but it's hard to live there. You have to dig through piles before you find the shirt you want. And sooner or later everything starts to smell bad.

The problem with having a sloppy life is that it keeps us from really living. Don't let a bunch of stuff get in the way of living with Jesus in your house.

Make it so:

Once during this Adventure, set aside a block of time to take out the trash in your life. Examine your life for attitudes, behaviors, or involvements that do not please God. If there are physical objects associated with these sins—magazines, CDs, posters, drugs, alcohol, etc.—take a trash bag and throw the objects away.

If there is no specific object involved, see if you can find a symbolic object. If pride is your problem, throw out a mirror. You get the idea. If you can't think of a symbolic object, simply write down the behavior that's messing up your life. Then destroy the paper in some meaningful way.

If you are deciding to discard a bad aspect of a relationship—lust, jealousy, anger—see if you can work with the other person to eliminate your sin together.

As you do this, and after, pray that Jesus will help you follow him more closely.

(Note: Some of the trash you need to throw out may be too much to handle by yourself. Consider finding others who can support you, hold you accountable, and check up on you.)

warm-up

friday, date

1. Paul has been talking about reaching the whole world with the Good News about Jesus—not just the *chosen few.* What's on Paul's wish list for his friends?

2. What on this wish list would you also put on <u>your</u> wish list?

3. What is on your wish list for your church that's not on Paul's? I wish . . . (Choose as many as you like.)

❑ This year's youth group ski trip were in the Alps.

❑ The pastor would preach 30-second sermons in church.

❑ The church would pay my college tuition.

❑ There could be a mosh pit in front of the pulpit.

❑ Everybody mattered and I belonged.

❑ I could feel comfortable bringing my friends.

❑ It would be okay to be me.

❑ We would help each other be all we can be.

❑ People were real.

❑ We could make a difference in the world.

❑ God showed up more often.

❑ The future looked bright.

4. If there were no rules and you were king, what would you ask for your church that seems beyond imagining?

5. In a more practical way, how would you like to turn your church inside out?

6. Why do you think Paul asked God for help instead of just telling his friends what to do?

unanswered Questions

Read 1 Peter 2:9-12.

Peter was writing to Christians who probably didn't have a church building to meet in. If they were going to act as a church, it wouldn't be because of their address, but because of their behavior.

1. According to this passage, what have you done to deserve being chosen by God? (Trick question. The answer is, nothing.)

2. This passage tells a story in three parts. From the text fill in the blanks.
What you were:
What you are:
What you need to do now:

3. Think of someone you know who is anti-Christian. In that person's mind, what is bad about being a Christian? What is good?
Bad:
Good:

4. Ask three non-Christian friends what they think about church or Christians. Record their responses.
1.
2.
3.

5. Fill in what's hot about being a Christian and what's not.

Hot	Not

6. What, if anything, can you do to improve the image of Christianity?

unanswered questions

theme 1
Everybody Matters

What if someone important were to show up at your next youth group meeting? The president. Michael Jordan. Even Sandra Bullock.

You would bend over backward to meet the needs of that celebrity, wouldn't you? *Is your chair comfortable? Can you see clearly? Would you like me to massage your feet?*

And what if that person wanted to talk about some personal concerns? Sandra has to decide which megablockbuster hit to star in next; Michael's worried because it's been a while since he's scored 50; the president wonders whether he really has what it takes to be the leader of the Free World.

Would you listen? Of course! You would feel honored that they had chosen you, and your youth group, to confide in. You would hang on every word. You would offer to pray with these people. And you would be happy to go out for coffee and talk some more.

Well (and you can see this point coming from a mile away, can't you?), someone important <u>has been</u> coming to your youth group meetings. In fact, everyone there is important. And how do you treat him or her?

Love to chat, but I've got to run home and study calculus.

Look, I know you're, like, suicidal right now, but could you hurry it up? <u>Seinfeld</u> is on in a half hour.

Here's a quarter. Call somebody who cares. On second thought, I need that quarter. Call 1-800-COLLECT.

Why do we treat other people like that? Because we're focused on our own needs and we don't want to be bothered with their concerns. We're struggling to find our own way in the world, our own identity, and we're afraid that others might drag us down. We don't want to be associated with losers, so we avoid the people who seem to have the most needs. Sometimes we try to be nice about it, but we still avoid them. We tune them out.

Our music is cranked up so loud, that we can't hear the doorbell ring. But if we opened the door, we might find a celebrity standing there—Jesus.

When Jesus Christ is in the house, it stops being <u>every man for himself</u> and becomes <u>all for one and one for all.</u>

True story. Jesus was walking along a city street and crowds were following him, clamoring for his attention. A blind beggar by the side of the road called out to Jesus. In the middle of all that noise, Jesus heard the blind man's cry and stopped to talk with him. When Jesus left, the man could see.

Jesus was always dealing with needs everyone else ignored. The disciples tried to shoo away some children, but Jesus said, *Let them come to me.* He stood up for a woman caught in the act of adultery, and he hung out with the outcasts of society.

What's more, he urges us to do the same. In one of his parables, he said, *What you do for the <u>little people</u>—the ones everyone else ignores—you do for me.* (Read it for yourself in Matthew 25:31–46.)

When we have serious concerns and needs, we want others to listen, to support, to help. As we follow Christ, we learn to do the same for others.

When Jesus Christ is in the house, it becomes a house of love.

Looking Back

Check the box if you have completed the assignment.
- ☐ I read the introductory material on pages 3–12.
- ☐ I read the introduction in I Like Church, But...
- ☐ I completed the warm-up days on pages 13–14.
- ☐ I read page 15 (Everybody Matters).

moving forward

Theme 1:

When Jesus is in the house, it's a place where everybody matters.

Assignments for This Week:
- Read chapter 1 in I Like Church, But...
- Rave to a friend about your youth group or church (Action Step 2, p. 8).

Daily Assignments:
- Read the assigned Scripture passages and answer the questions in the journal.
- Pray the Pierced Ears Prayer (Action Step 1, pp. 6–7).
- Write down something good about your youth group or church on page 40 (Action Step 2, p. 8).

Still to Come:
- Get together with two people outside your normal circle of friends (Action Step 3, p. 9).
- Invite someone to youth group or church (Action Step 2, p. 8).
- Help bring out a friend's potential (Action Step 4, p. 11).
- Take out the trash in your life (Action Step 5, p. 12).

A Resource for This 50-Day Adventure:
I Like Church, But... by Dan Lupton (Guidebook or Audio Guidebook)

In addition to your journals each household needs one copy of the Adventure Guidebook. This essential, easy-to-read book includes a chapter for each of the eight Adventure themes. In it you'll find:

- Motivational insights and inspiration.   • In-depth theme explanations.
- Practical helps and illustrations.   • Additional action step suggestions.

Ask for this resource at your church or local Christian bookstore, or call The Chapel Ministries at 1-800-224-2735.

day 1

Sunday, date

Read Acts 2:42-47; 4:32-35.

From: ThunderOne
To: RockMan
great sermon peter but what are we gonna do with all these people??? :-&
        John

 **What's the 411**

Many of the new believers in the early church were from other towns. Some of them had been disowned by their families, so the physical needs of these believers were a high priority.

1. If you made a movie of the scene in Acts 2, what would you call it?

Enough is Enough

2. What things did these Christians do together? How did they care for each other?

Ate, prayed, broke bread, praised God, did miracles, They gave to anyone who had need

3. How do you think the average person in the early church felt about selling possessions to care for the needy?
- ☒ Anything I can do to help.   ☒ I'm sure going to miss my donkey.
- ☐ You owe me, man.   ☐ Other [   ]

4. How would you feel if you saw this sort of thing happening at your church? How would you respond?

That it was kind, but it'd be hard for me to do.

5. If a group of needy people like this came to your church, what could you do?
- ☒ Take up an offering.   ☒ Make sure they have places to stay.   ☒ Find jobs for them.
- ☐ Wash their feet.   ☒ Feed them.   ☐ Take them to a movie.
- ☐ Call someone who cares.   ☐ Other [   ]

6. What would be the hardest thing for you to give up for the well-being of someone else?
- ☒ CD collection   ☒ Computer   ☐ TV   ☐ Homework   ☐ Chores
- ☒ Car   ☐ Snowboard, surfboard, or skateboard   ☐ Other [   ]

Unanswered Questions

17

Read Mark 10:46–52.

 What's the **411**

Here is a roadside encounter between Jesus and a seriously needy guy. Coincidence? Think again.

1. What was the response of most people to Bartimaeus's cry?

2. Bartimaeus was someone whom everyone else passed by without noticing, yet he mattered to Jesus. How does it make you feel to know that Jesus listened to someone whom everyone else disregarded? Why?

3. Why do you think Jesus asked Bartimaeus, *What do you want me to do for you?*

4. How would you answer if Jesus asked you the same question?
☐ What Bart said.
☐ I'd like good looks, fame, and fortune, please.
☐ I just want a good heart.
☐ Could you pay my college tuition?
☐ How about a date with Chris O'Donnell/Alicia Silverstone?
☐ I'll take a double cappuccino.
☐ Other [   ]

5. Do you know someone like Bartimaeus who often is overlooked? What do you think his or her answer would be to Jesus' question?

6. How can you know what people need? How can you make sure that everyone matters to you?

unanswered Questions

day 3
tuesday,
date

Read Romans 12:9–16.

 What's the 4 1 1   Paul's just been talking about the Christian's obligation to give his or her life to Jesus and allow it to be transformed. What's next?

1. List Paul's instructions. (Hint: check for the verbs. We counted 18 or so. How many can you find?)

2. Look through your list and underline everything you like someone else to do for you. Put a box around the things that are easiest for you to do. Circle what you think is the hardest command to follow.

3. What is one thing from the list you can start working on this week?

4. How could following these instructions make your church or youth group a caring place where everyone matters?

5. Pick a number between 1 and 8. Add 8. Go to that verse. If everyone in your church or youth group put this single verse into practice, what changes would you expect to see?

unanswered Questions

Read 1 John 4:7–12.

What's the 411

The opening part of yesterday's passage talked about how love must be sincere. These verses tell us what love is. And actions speak louder than words.

KEYWORD

<u>Atoning sacrifice</u>—When one person pays a debt owed by another.

1. According to this passage, love is ...
- ☐ Never having to say you're sorry.
- ☐ God sending Jesus to die for our sins.
- ☐ What we do because God loved us.
- ☐ A sign that we truly know God.
- ☐ Zero in the game of tennis.
- ☐ Other [_____]

2. You've been praying the Pierced Ears Prayer each day, asking for God to help you respond to the needs of others. What needs have you heard recently? How might you respond to these?

3. How does verse 9 say God showed his love for us?

4. With this in mind, how might you be able to show love in your church, your youth group, or among your friends?

Unanswered Questions

Read 2 Samuel 9:1–10.

Jonathan and David were best friends. Even though Jonathan was the son of King Saul and should have been next in line to be king, he supported David as God's chosen leader. David never forgot Jonathan's love and friendship, and promised to always care for his family. (See 1 Samuel 20:11–17.) Today's reading takes place after Jonathan's death.

1. At the beginning of this passage, what was David's quest? What did he do for Mephibosheth?

2. Why did Mephibosheth need help?

3. If Mephibosheth were to write a thank-you note to King David, what would it say?

Dear King David,

unanswered Questions

day 6.
friday,
date

Read Philippians 2:1–4.

Paul's been talking about good behavior that should accompany the Good News about Jesus.

1. Make your own list of contrasting behaviors based on Paul's comments. We've given you an example to get you started.

Treat others better	Treat self better
Example: Respect people	Use people

Now you try:

Treat others better	Treat self better
Listen a lot	_____
_____	Get what you want
Make people happy Tune in to people's needs	_____
_____	Always be right
Take risks to help people	_____

2. Of your waking hours, what percentage of time do you spend thinking about others? What percentage do you spend thinking about yourself? Use the clocks below as pie charts. Shade the portion of your waking hours that you . . .

Think of others.

Think of yourself.

This passage is not about beating yourself up. It's a Golden Rule thing.

3. Is there anything in this list that you should be working on? What can you do to start making that happen? Who could help you?

unanswered Questions

It's getting late, I gotta go. I have to go to church in the morning.

    Church? You?

    Yeah. Ya know—parents. Wish I could sleep, but ya gotta do what ya gotta do.

    Well, see you later.

    Hey, I almost forgot. Tomorrow is Bring-a-Friend Sunday. You wanna come?

Of course not! You're making your church sound about as exciting as flossing your teeth. Why would <u>anyone</u> want to come?

You see, we're guilty of a conspiracy. We Christians (well, most of us anyway) have been keeping a secret. It hasn't always been easy, but we've managed to keep this bit of info pretty well under wraps. Here's the secret: Jesus Christ is in the house.

If people really knew this, we'd have all sorts of folks barging into our churches—we wouldn't be able to keep them away. Church wouldn't be just for us anymore.

Yet, if you were to poll your classmates about their favorite activities, church would rank down there around Accordion Night at the VFW. Maybe it's time we let people in on our secret.

There are two possible problems here:

1. <u>We've forgotten the secret ourselves.</u> There are people who've been doing church for so long that they've lost sight of the fact that Jesus is in the house. Church is boring for these people because they've forgotten why they're there. Even your youth group may be drowning in a sea of icebreakers (or frozen in a dry ice of lectures).

2. <u>We are keeping the secret from outsiders.</u> Maybe your church is great. Maybe your youth group is fine. And maybe you just bad-mouth the church because, well, because that's what your friends expect to hear.

If that's the case, then you're guilty of a cover-up worse than anything Nixon ever tried. If your friends expect church to be dull, then surprise them with the truth. Dare them to try it for themselves.

The psalmist said, *I rejoiced with those who said to me, 'Let us go to the house of the Lord.'* When Jesus Christ is in the house, why would anyone want to be anywhere else?

When we wake up and smell the secret of Christ's presence, things change.

• Now we do church to meet our living Lord, not for that perfect-attendance pin.

• Now our services are hopping with the praises of our hearts, not drifting off in the fifth stanza of a hymn from long ago and far away.

• Now we use real language to express our love for the Lord and each other, language that newcomers can understand, not the pious phrases that set us apart.

• Now we can welcome visitors to join in our worship, to encounter our enjoyable Lord with us, and not just to be another tally in our attendance count.

If your church seems to have forgotten the secret, do what you can to remind it. If your youth group ignores the presence of Christ, there's probably even more you can do. Talk it up. Bust this secret wide open.

Looking Back

Check the box if you have completed the assignment.

☐ I read chapter 1 in I Like Church, But...
☐ I completed Days 1–6.
☐ I prayed the Pierced Ears Prayer.
☐ I wrote down good things about my youth group or church.
☐ I raved to a friend about my youth group or church.
☐ I read page 23 (You Can Bring Your Friends).

moving forward

Theme 2:

When Jesus is in the house, it's a place where you can bring your friends.

Assignments for This Week:
• Read chapter 2 in I Like Church, But...
• Rave to a friend about your youth group or church (Action Step 2, p. 8).

Daily Assignments:
• Read the assigned Scripture passages and answer the questions in the journal.
• Pray the Pierced Ears Prayer (Action Step 1, pp. 6–7).
• Write down something good about your youth group or church on page 40 (Action Step 2, p. 8).

Before the End:
• Invite someone to youth group or church (Action Step 2, p. 8).

Still to Come:
• Get together with two people outside your normal circle of friends (Action Step 3, p. 9).
• Help bring out a friend's potential (Action Step 4, p. 11).
• Take out the trash in your life (Action Step 5, p. 12).

theme 2:
You Can Bring Your Friends

Read Acts 5:12-16.

From: RockMan
To: ThunderOne
everything's rockin :-) in the colonnade these days but there's something strange—people keep following me around, especially on sunny days—why is that?
+-:-) Peter

 **What's the 411** The story of the First Church of Jerusalem continues.

1. You are an on-the-street reporter in Jerusalem asking people what they think of this new group—the Christians. Write down three responses you might expect from the average person on the street.

1.
2.
3.

2. What do you think the church was doing to make themselves *highly regarded by the people*?

3. How is your church/youth group (choose one) regarded by the people in your community/school (choose one)?
- ❏ What church/youth group?
- ❏ Old-fashioned
- ❏ A great place to visit
- ❏ Holier-than-thou
- ❏ Free pizza!
- ❏ Great place to meet guys/girls
- ❏ They care about people
- ❏ A place to go if you're in trouble
- ❏ Don't you have to be rich to go there?
- ❏ Other [   ]

4. What is your youth group like?
- ❏ Dangerous
- ❏ Inviting
- ❏ Stupid
- ❏ Free
- ❏ Other [   ]

unanswered Questions

theme 2
You Can Bring Your Friends

Read Matthew 5:13–16.

day 9!
monday,
date

We join the Sermon on the Mount already in progress. Salt was a preservative as well as a seasoning during New Testament times. It was so valuable people were often paid in salt.

1. Choose one of the following and finish the paragraph in your own words.

You are the ketchup of the earth . . .

You are the beeper of the earth . . .

You are the skateboard . . .

You are the Internet . . .

You are the . . .

2. Do you find it true that people glorify God because of the good deeds of others? Explain your answer.

3. Why do you think Jesus used the image of light in this sermon?

❑ Light helps people see better.

❑ Light travels fast.

❑ Because some people sleep with a night-light.

❑ Lasers look really cool.

❑ Light protects people from crime.

❑ It's not too heavy.

❑ Light is energy.

❑ Other [   ]

4. If you had your way, what effect would your church, youth group, or group of friends have on your community?

5. What can you do to let your light shine?

unanswered questions

26

Read Acts 9:36–43.

From: Dorc
To: RockMan
can't thank you enough for that ticket back to earth last week X-(, the ladies are still talking about it—anyway i'm just catching up on my sewing then it's back to the thrift shop part-time. :-o (when i asked my boss for a raise that's not what i had in mind! :->)
Ta Ta, Tabitha

 What's the 411 The young church has busted out of Jerusalem.

1. What was Tabitha's reputation in the community?

2. How would you have responded if you were in the room when Peter presented Tabitha—alive?

☐ You again. ☐ This is a trick, right?

☐ Good. Now she can make me a new toga.

☐ There must be something to this Christianity stuff.

☐ You again. ☐ Praise the Lord. ☐ Me next.

☐ I told you not to cash that life insurance check.

☐ Other [   ]

3. What two things would sum up your rep at school?

1.

2.

4. How does your personal rep affect the rep of your church or youth group?

Unanswered Questions

theme 2
You Can Bring Your
Friends

day 11
wednesday,
date

Read Philippians 2:14-16.

1. What was the last complaint you heard from someone in your church or youth group?

2. How does complaining and arguing keep us from being blameless and pure?

3. Be an artist and create illustrations for these captions.

This is your soul.   This is your soul when you complain too much.

4. What can you or your group do to shine like stars in the universe? Do you really want to do this? Explain.

5. In what ways should you stand out from nonbelievers around you? In what ways should your church or youth group stand out?

unanswered Questions

day 12
thursday,
date

theme 2
You Can Bring Your Friends

Read John 4:1-30, 39-42.

What's the 411   Zero in on verse 28.

1. Why do you think the Samaritans went to see Jesus?

2. If you told others about your encounter with Jesus, what would you say? Come see a man . . .

3. Fill in the balloons below with what your non-Christian friends would say if they came to church or youth group with you.

4. Would you be afraid or embarrassed to invite a friend to church or youth group? Explain.

5. What can you do to make your church or youth group a place where you would want to bring your friends—or even where they would ask to come?

unanswered Questions

theme 2
You Can Bring Your Friends

day 13
friday,
date

Read 2 Kings 5:1-15.

 Elisha, God's prophet, has been causing quite a stir.

1. How did Naaman find out about the prophet who could heal him?

What's the 411 This *young* girl was probably your age or younger, yet she made a big difference.

2. Why do you think Naaman took the trouble to journey into enemy territory to see this prophet?

3. Alex's parents are getting divorced. Sheryl is lonely. Vanessa feels guilty all the time. Tyrone can't concentrate. Ashley has an eating disorder. John has a problem with drugs and alcohol. What can you or your group do to help these people?

4. How does your church respond to needy people?
- ❑ God must be punishing them.
  - ❑ If they worked harder, they wouldn't be needy.
  - ❑ This is a problem-free world.
    - ❑ Come on in. We'll set another place at the table.
- ❑ Would you like fries with that?
  - ❑ How can we help?
- ❑ Other [   ]

unanswered Questions

theme 3
It's Okay to Be Me.

UBU. No, I'm not talking about a new reggae band or a rare Himalayan monkey. This was a slogan that appeared a few years ago in an ad for some trendy manufacturer.

Those three letters express a philosophy of life. U B U. Be yourself. You don't have to squeeze into anyone else's mold.

Sounds good, but you're actually playing roles all the time, aren't you? You have to convince your teachers you're a serious scholar. You work at persuading your parents you're a model child. And how much time do you put into convincing the opposite sex that you're cooler, more confident, and better looking than you really are?

Wouldn't it be great to find a group of people who accept you for who you are, regardless of your grades, looks, or zip code?

The church could be like that. It should be like that, but unfortunately that's not always the case. Some churches have unwritten rules about how you should dress, how you should speak, or even how much money you should put in the plate. If you don't fit into the mold, you're given the cold shoulder.

But how welcoming is your youth group? And how accepting are you? How do you treat the kid who shows up with zero fashion sense, too many (or too few) body piercings, or smelly no-name sneakers? Do you reach across boundaries to befriend people of other races, other cultures, other languages, other ages, other levels of income?

The church—and your youth group—will become a more accepting place when you become a more accepting person. You need to cross the lines.

In the early church there were Jews and Gentiles. Most Jewish Christians had been given good Bible training as they grew up. They knew the laws of God and the prophecies about the Messiah. They were generally good, moral people.

But then the Good News of Jesus was shared with the Gentiles, the non-Jews. Most of these people knew little or nothing about the Scriptures. They had been brought up in homes that practiced all sorts of crazy lifestyles. When they accepted Jesus, they committed themselves to a new kind of life, but they still did and said a lot of things that the Jewish Christians considered inappropriate.

This was one of the biggest problems in the early church. Some Jewish Christians tried to make the Gentile Christians adopt all the Jewish ways, but the apostle Paul insisted that this was not necessary. As long as they honored Christ, the Gentiles could be a bit different. They didn't have to try to be what they weren't.

Nowadays we have church people and *unchurched* people, those who know the Bible and those who don't. Sometimes church people behave as if they really don't want outsiders to come to church—unless they first learn how to do all the *churchy things*. As a result, everyone gets the message: Church is not a place where I can be myself.

The message of Scripture is a different one: *But now in Christ Jesus you who once were far away have been brought near through the blood of Christ. For he himself is our peace, who has made the two one and has destroyed the barrier. . . . He came and preached peace to you who were far away and peace to those who were near. For through him we both have access to the Father by one Spirit* (Ephesians 2:13–14, 17–18).

When Jesus Christ is in the house, there is no division. He welcomes all sorts of people into a relationship with him.

Looking Back

Check the box if you have completed the assignment.

- ☐ I read chapter 2 in I Like Church, But...
- ☐ I completed Days 7–13.
- ☐ I prayed the Pierced Ears Prayer.
- ☐ I wrote down good things about my youth group or church.
- ☐ I raved to a friend about my youth group or church.
- ☐ I invited someone to youth group or church.
- ☐ I read page 31 (It's Okay to Be Me).

moving forward

Theme 3:

When Jesus is in the house, it's a place where it's okay to be me.

Assignments for This Week:

- Read chapter 3 in I Like Church, But...
- Rave to a friend about your youth group or church (Action Step 2, p. 8).

Daily Assignments:

- Read the assigned Scripture passages and answer the questions in the journal.
- Pray the Pierced Ears Prayer (Action Step 1, pp. 6–7).
- Write down something good about your youth group or church on page 40 (Action Step 2, p. 8).

Before the End:

- Invite someone to youth group or church (Action Step 2, p. 8).
- Get together with two people outside your normal circle of friends (Action Step 3, p. 9).

Still to Come:

- Help bring out a friend's potential (Action Step 4, p. 11).
- Take out the trash in your life (Action Step 5, p. 12).

Read Acts 10:1-35.

From: RockMan
To: Churion@rome.emp.mil

sorry it took so long to answer your email but i wasn't sure if my religion allowed contact with romans—then I had this dream—wild :-0 let's just say i'll never look at a pork chop the same way again. :-*

so anyway i'd be happy to come and talk to you about JESUS. how's this weekend look to you? sure you're not out pillaging a village or something? just a little army joke, there, sir. :-)

CU soon,

+-:-) Peter

KEYWORD

<u>Unclean</u>—Any Old Testament classification of food, people, practices, and so on, that Jews were to avoid.

1. How did Peter feel when he heard the voice telling him to eat *unclean* food?

2. Why did Peter welcome the Gentile visitors and go to meet Cornelius?

3. Peter had to cross the lines in order to obey God. God wanted the Gentiles to hear the Good News also. What are the lines that you find tough to cross?

☐ Race ☐ Sex ☐ Financial status ☐ Popularity ☐ Clique ☐ Disability

☐ Religion ☐ Lifestyle ☐ Other _____

4. How might God ask you to cross the line?

☐ Invite the person to church. ☐ Have lunch with the person. ☐ Talk with the person.

☐ Stand up for the person. ☐ Find out the person's needs you can meet.

☐ Other _____

unanswered Questions

theme 3
It's Okay to Be Me

day 16,
monday,
date

Read Leviticus 19:32-34.

 Aliens in this case aren't space invaders, but foreigners.

1. How are God's people supposed to treat the elderly?

2. How are God's people supposed to treat foreigners?

3. How would you describe the attitude most of your friends show toward people older than you? Toward those who don't fit in?

4. Who would you consider the aliens (outsiders) in your community?

5. Each thing that separates you from the elderly and foreigners in your community is like a brick. If you collect enough such *bricks,* soon you'll have a wall. In the bricks in the wall below, list all the things that tend to prevent you from getting to know elderly and foreign people better.

unanswered Questions

Read James 2:1-9.

1. How would a poorly dressed person feel in your church or youth group? Why?

2. What status symbols get the attention of your church, youth group, community, or school? (Check all that apply.)

- ☐ Doc Martens
- ☐ Starter jacket
- ☐ Tommy
- ☐ Goodwill
- ☐ Big hair
- ☐ Nose ring
- ☐ No hair
- ☐ Swimming pool
- ☐ Gold
- ☐ Beeper/cell phone
- ☐ Snowboard
- ☐ Colors
- ☐ Country club
- ☐ Team jersey
- ☐ 4-Runner
- ☐ Blackflyes
- ☐ Cash
- ☐ Gold card
- ☐ Game
- ☐ Private school
- ☐ Other [   ]

3. Why do you think God takes equal treatment of others so seriously?

4. In what ways do _you_ show favoritism? What can you do to improve your treatment of others?

unanswered Questions

35

Read Romans 14:1–12.

 What's the 411 — Paul was writing to Christians who were mad at each other for all the wrong reasons and were arguing over all kinds of differences.

1. According to this passage how important are the following issues? (1=unimportant, 10=very important.)
• Eating only veggies _____
• Observing holy days _____
• Giving thanks to God _____

2. How important do you think these issues are? (Use the same scale.)
• How nicely you dress for church _____
• Predestination _____
• Whether Christians should go to movies _____
• Baptism by sprinkling or dunking _____
• Working on the Sabbath _____
• Drums in church _____
• Whether Christians should watch *Married . . . with Children* _____
• Whether you're a Republican or Democrat _____

3. What other issues do Christians disagree about today?

4. Often Christians build walls between themselves and other Christians because they disagree over matters that have little to do with basic belief in Christ. Are there ways that you can cross this line without violating clear teachings of Scripture?

5. Have you ever looked down on someone who calls Jesus Lord because the person expressed his or her faith differently than you? Explain. If yes, what is the first step you need to take to make peace with the person?

Unanswered Questions

theme 3
It's Okay to Be Me

Read Acts 9:19b–28.

From: BigBro
To: BarnDoor

sorry barnabas we're still getting used to this churchnet here and something caused some mix-up in the file—we thought you said you wanted to bring **SAUL** to our next meeting. ;-) that would be a good one :-p so please re-send that last message and we'll try to keep our wires straight.

James

Before he was the apostle Paul, our hero was a militant rabbi named Saul. The young Christian church was understandably cautious.

1. How did the disciples react to Saul's attempts to join them? Why?

2. Why do you think Barnabas had the guts to take a chance on Saul?

3. What kinds of people are others afraid of welcoming today (ex-cons, people with AIDS, unwed mothers, etc.)? How do you think Christ wants the church to respond to these people?

4. Let's say you get to vote on church membership. All the applicants have professed their faith in Jesus Christ. How easy would it be (on a scale of 1–10; 1=hard ,10=easy) to approve the following people?
- Drunk driver who killed your best friend _____
- Former Klansman _____
- Convicted rapist _____
- Admitted child molester _____
- Other [   ] _____

5. Of all the kinds of people you can think of, who would be hardest for you to accept as a Christian brother or sister?

unanswered Questions

Read Revelation 7:9-10.

What's the 411

The apostle John has been invited to peer into the future, and he's got heaven on his mind. Here he's talking about who's in the house.

1. Who's in this multitude? What are they doing and saying?

2. Who else is in this multitude? (Check all that apply.)

☐ You ☐ Different races ☐ Different ethnic groups
☐ Men ☐ Women ☐ Young people ☐ Middle-aged people
☐ Older people ☐ People in different financial classes ☐ Popular people
☐ Unpopular people ☐ People with disabilities ☐ People with different lifestyles
☐ Outsiders ☐ Poorly dressed people ☐ People of low status
☐ People without much talent ☐ Poor people ☐ Rich people
☐ Christians with whom you disagree ☐ Ex-cons
☐ People with AIDS ☐ Unwed mothers ☐ Drunk drivers ☐ Former Klansmen
☐ Convicted rapists ☐ Admitted child molesters ☐ Murderers ☐ Your parents
☐ Your friends ☐ Extroverts ☐ Introverts ☐ Homeless people
☐ Other [   ]

3. What can Christians do to facilitate this kind of unity and praise <u>before</u> we get to heaven?

unanswered Questions

Every spring, I (Randy) direct the musical at my old high school. Though it's a lot of work, and things can get pretty tense the week before we open, I love the whole experience.

I get a chance to work with some very talented people. But the thing is, many of them don't realize how talented they are. And what I love most about directing is helping people do things they didn't know they could do.

Lauren had played supporting roles for several years, but last year, as a senior, she landed a major part in Carousel—the conniving carousel owner, Mrs. Mullin. In our early rehearsals, we worked on her character, trying to figure out why Mrs. Mullin did and said what she did and said. Lauren was a smart girl who understood the character very well, but she was still not saying her lines as effectively as she could.

As the director, I really didn't do much except give her permission to *push the envelope,* to try some new things. I think she might have been afraid to make a mistake, so she was holding back a little. *Go for it,* I told her. *Be as strong as you can be in this scene. Don't hold back.*

That was all she needed. She turned in a stunning performance, surprising everyone (including herself) with the strength and maturity of her portrayal. I couldn't take much credit for it. In fact, I really hadn't spent much time telling her what to do. I just encouraged her to be all she could be. I gave her permission to do what she already had the ability to do.

Every actor is a bit different. Eric played the lead, Billy Bigelow, and he nailed it. He got better and better as he relaxed. My job was to give him the confidence he needed.

Stephanie had natural comic timing, but I had to sculpt her performance in a way: *Pull back on this, but try this.* With Brad and Ryan, I tried to give them a vision of their characters—smarmy or straight-laced. With Jessica, an actress of deep emotion, it was a matter of identifying the feelings of her character in each scene and letting her capture the heart of the heroine, Julie Jordan.

I don't mean to bore you with this artsy drama talk, but I want to give you a picture of the kind of influence one person can have on others. At every audition, I have to choose actors with the potential to do a great job on stage. But every day you're moving among friends who have potential to do incredible things in life.

Sometimes they just need permission to try something. *You really should go out for the team. You're really good.*

Sometimes they need some *sculpting.* *Try this instead of that.*

Sometimes they're already involved in something, but they need to relax to do it well. You can give them the encouragement they need.

Sometimes you need to give them a vision of where they could go with the talents they have. *You really could get a scholarship and go to a top college. Why don't you apply?*

(continued on p. 42)

a few goo

In the spaces provided, write some good things about your church or youth group.

Day 1 _____
Day 2 _____
Day 3 _____
Day 4 _____
Day 5 _____
Day 6 _____

Day 7 _____
Day 8 _____
Day 9 _____
Day 10 _____
Day 11 _____
Day 12 _____
Day 13 _____

Day 14 _____
Day 15 _____
Day 16 _____
Day 17 _____
Day 18 _____
Day 19 _____
Day 20 _____

Day 21 _____
Day 22 _____
Day 23 _____
Day 24 _____
Day 25 _____

 d w:Ords

more information on Action Step 2—Catch the Rave—see page 8.

Day 26 _____

Day 27 _____

Day 28 _____

Day 29 _____

Day 30 _____

Day 31 _____

Day 32 _____

Day 33 _____

Day 34 _____

Day 35 _____

Day 36 _____

Day 37 _____

Day 38 _____

Day 39 _____

Day 40 _____

Day 41 _____

Day 42 _____

Day 43 _____

Day 44 _____

Day 45 _____

Day 46 _____

Day 47 _____

Day 48 _____

Day 49 _____

Day 50 _____

We Help Each Other Be All We Can Be

(continued from p. 39)

In the Bible, Barnabas did all of these things and more. In fact, Barnabas is actually a nickname his friends gave him—it means *The Encouragement Guy.* I like to think of him as a director.

When no one else would dare cast Saul in the role of *Christian missionary,* Barnabas gave him a chance to be a star. Later, when young John Mark was about to be cut from the cast, Barnabas stood up for him and kept him in the production. The Encouragement Guy even used his own money to make sure the show would go on.

The Bible says that God has given special abilities to every Christian. And what are these abilities for? *To prepare God's people for works of service, so that the body of Christ may be built up* (Ephesians 4:12). So, whatever your ability is, you should use it to help other Christians find and use their own abilities. As we help each other, the body of Christ (the church) grows strong.

When Jesus Christ is in the house, we want to perform well for him. But we're not just solo performers—we're a team. We work together to develop each other's gifts so we all can join the cast and put on a great show for God's glory.

Looking Back

Check the box if you have completed the assignment.

- ❏ I read chapter 3 in I Like Church, But...
- ❏ I completed Days 14–20.
- ❏ I prayed the Pierced Ears Prayer.
- ❏ I wrote down good things about my youth group or church.
- ❏ I raved to a friend about my youth group or church.
- ❏ I invited someone to youth group or church.
- ❏ I got together with two people outside my circle.
- ❏ I read pages 39 and 42 (We Help Each Other Be All We Can Be).

moving forward

Theme 4:

When Jesus is in the house, it's a place where we help each other be all we can be.

Assignments for This Week:

- Read chapter 4 in I Like Church, But...
- Rave to a friend about your youth group or church (Action Step 2, p. 8).

Daily Assignments:

- Read the assigned Scripture passages and answer the questions in the journal.
- Pray the Pierced Ears Prayer (Action Step 1, pp. 6–7).
- Write down something good about your youth group or church on pages 40–41 (Action Step 2, p. 8).

Before the End:

- Invite someone to youth group or church (Action Step 2, p. 8).
- Get together with two people outside your normal circle of friends (Action Step 3, p. 9).
- Help bring out a friend's potential (Action Step 4, p. 11).

Still to Come:

- Take out the trash in your life (Action Step 5, p. 12).

theme 4
We Help Each Other
Be All We Can Be

day 21/22
saturday/sunday
dates

Read Acts 18:24-26.

From: Tentmakers
To: Speakeasy
apollos—we've been following some of your postings and they're very well done but there seems to be a problem. no offense but it looks like you've only downloaded half the file—john's baptism is good but it was just the start. we can tell you so much more. find us in the chat room under KEYWORD: JESUS. P+A

 What's the 411

Paul is all over the map, leading people to Jesus. Meanwhile, a Jewish guy from Egypt shows up in Ephesus with a powerful and persuasive message—the trouble is, he doesn't know what he doesn't know.

WHOIS

Priscilla and Aquila were a husband-and-wife team who took Paul into their tentmaking business when he preached in Corinth. Eighteen months later, Paul returned the favor by taking them on the road with him. Paul left Priscilla and Aquila to help the Christians in Ephesus.

1. Who was Apollos?

2. How did Priscilla and Aquila help Apollos become a better preacher?

3. What do you think would've happened if Priscilla and Aquila had never helped Apollos?
- ☐ Someone else would have.
- ☐ Apollos would have led people astray.
- ☐ Lots of people would never have heard the whole gospel.
- ☐ Tent production would have increased.
- ☐ The entire space-time continuum would have been disrupted.
- ☐ Other [   ]

4. In this Adventure, you'll be choosing someone like Apollos whom you can help to serve God better. What tips can you learn from Priscilla and Aquila about how to help somebody like this?

unanswered Questions

day 23
monday,
date

Read Matthew 9:9-13.

Apart from this story, we don't know much about Matthew. He did write this gospel, which emphasizes that Jesus was the fulfillment of Old Testament promises. Hmmm, so even though Matthew was despised by the religious leaders, he knew their Scriptures (or he learned them from Jesus). Maybe Jesus saw that Matthew was bright and teachable.

WHOIS

Pharisees—These guys were at the center of Jewish religion in the first century. Some of them tried very hard to please God as they understood him, but many had become self-righteous control freaks who made life very hard for everyone else.
Tax collectors—It's a long way from Rome to Jerusalem, so the Romans hired local contractors to collect their taxes. The tax collectors had the same kind of reputation that mobsters have in modern America—they were very rich and very unpopular with their neighbors.

1. Why do you think Jesus chose Matthew as a disciple?
- ❏ Matthew was wearing a *Choose Me* T-shirt.
- ❏ Matthew would know some valuable tax loopholes.
- ❏ Matthew would know other tax collectors, and they threw the best parties.
- ❏ As a former tax collector, Matthew could count the money from offerings.
- ❏ As a tax collector, Matthew would know how to write, and might even write a gospel.
- ❏ Because Mark and Luke were on vacation.
- ❏ Other [   ]

2. Who are the *tax collectors* today? We're talking about people who are looked down on by leaders or religious people. Are there kids at your school who get the same cold-shoulder treatment as first-century tax collectors? Jot down any names that come to mind.

3. Now, what can you do to help the people on your list:
Follow Jesus?

Use a talent to serve Jesus?

unanswered Questions

theme 4
We Help Each Other
Be All We Can Be

day 24
tuesday,
date

Read Philemon.

Paul writes this letter from prison to his friend Philemon and sends it by hand, and that hand belongs to Onesimus. The problem is that Onesimus once belonged to Philemon in one of those master/slave relationships, and he apparently had escaped. Now Paul is sending Onesimus back, asking Philemon to treat him like a brother instead of a slave. Everybody in this story has something to lose and something to gain.

1. How does Paul describe the slave Onesimus in this letter?

There is a pun in verse 11. The name Onesimus means *useful,* but he hadn't been very useful to his master Philemon. Yet after becoming a Christian, Onesimus was a changed man.

2. What does Paul ask Philemon to do for Onesimus the slave?

3. Do you think this is the way runaway slaves would normally be treated in those days? If not, what would you expect?

4. What risk was Paul taking here?
- ☐ If Onesimus caused trouble, Philemon might blame Paul.
- ☐ If word got around, all the slaves might run to see Paul.
- ☐ If the authorities found Paul being nice to a runaway, they might extend his sentence.
- ☐ Onesimus might get a better deal from the apostle Peter.
- ☐ Onesimus might run off with Paul's CD collection.
- ☐ This letter might be too short to get into the Bible.

5. Why do you think Paul chose to do this for Onesimus, putting his own rep on the line?

6. In this Adventure, you've been looking for someone like Onesimus, someone you can free up to be truly useful. What risks might you have to take in that person's behalf?

unanswered Questions

day 25
wednesday, date

theme 4
We Help Each Other
Be All We Can Be

Read Luke 8:1-3.

What's the 411

Ever get the impression that all the disciples of Jesus were men? Not so! In a world that was very hard on women, the women in this passage made important contributions to Christ's work in the world.

1. What role did these women have in Jesus' ministry?

2. If someone said to Jesus, *Wait a minute! These women can't be on your team because they're, well, female!* how do you think Jesus would respond?

Jesus' response

3. What do we learn about Mary Magdalene here?

4. If someone said to Jesus, *You can't possibly associate with this Mary woman; don't you know what troubles she has had in the past?* how do you think Jesus would've responded?

Jesus' response

What's the 411

Mary Magdalene was the first person Jesus appeared to after his resurrection.

5. As you look for someone to support and encourage as a part of Jesus' team, look for some Mary Magdalenes. Don't rule people out because they're male or female, too young, too white, disabled, socially challenged, or because they've had a bad past. Does this add any new names to your list of prospects?

unanswered Questions

day 26,
thursday,
date

Read 1 Samuel 16:1-13.

 The people of God demanded a king, and he turned out to be a bum. Now God gets in the act, sending Samuel to call the next king of Israel.

KEYWORD

Anointing—Putting ceremonial oil on people's heads was a big deal to the Jews. It symbolized the way God touches people so they can serve in ways that are better than what they could do on their own.

1. Why did Samuel go to Bethlehem?

2. Why do you think Samuel wanted to anoint Eliab, Jesse's oldest son?

3. Why didn't the Lord let him?

4. How do you think Jesse felt as the prophet passed up his seven oldest sons?

5. On a scale of 3 to 87, how much does *outward appearance* affect the way people at your school are treated?

3	19	31	53	68	87

(3) Not at all.
(19) Okay, maybe a little.
(31) It helps to look good, but we really prize inner qualities.
(53) All right, already! Looks are important, but not all-important.
(68) If you're not built and gorgeous, you'd better have brains or bucks.
(87) Babes and hunks only, please.

6. As God chooses people to serve him, how important is outward appearance?

3	19	31	53	68	87

Unanswered Questions

day 27
friday,
date

theme 4
We Help Each Other Be All We Can Be

Read Acts 4:1-14.

From: TGuard1
To: HiPriest

I understand your concern about this uprising of Jesus' followers but believe me—it won't amount to much. look at the people involved—most are galileans :-(they're fishermen. Even a tax collector. hardly the type to start a revolution.

Minutes earlier, Peter and John attracted a huge—and we might add, unauthorized—crowd because, in the name of Jesus, they healed a crippled guy. Everybody wanted to know what that was all about. Needless to say, the religious authorities were pretty uptight about it.

1. Why were Peter and John arrested?

2. Peter preached a great message in just a few sentences (verses 8–12). Let's say you want to download this message, but you only have room on your hard drive for 23 words. Cut this message down to 23 words so you can save it.

3. Which of the following conclusions can we draw from this passage?
- ❑ The best defense is a good offense.
- ❑ If you're a cop and you see some fishermen preaching and healing people, just leave them alone.
- ❑ If you don't have a seminary education, you can't say anything valuable about Jesus.
- ❑ It's Jesus who heals people; folks like Peter and John are just his servants.
- ❑ Watch out for unschooled, ordinary people. They may just turn the world upside down.
- ❑ The people we help are the strongest testimony to the truth of what we say.
- ❑ Other [   ]

4. As you look for someone to encourage, remember people like Peter and John—not the smartest or best educated, but people who are willing to risk it all for Jesus. Any new names come to mind?

unanswered Questions

You wouldn't catch me in church, not with all those hypocrites.
   Well, can you think of a better place for hypocrites to be?

   You've heard the criticism, haven't you? People have been throwing this at Christians for centuries, accusing us of being hypocrites, who judge others while going too easy on ourselves. All too often, we deserve it.

   You know what I'm talking about. They're just a bunch of phonies, going to church on Sunday so everyone can see how holy they are. Then on Monday they're lying and cheating like everyone else.
   Is that why people go to church? To show everyone how holy they are?
   Well, isn't it?

   And for some people, in some churches, that's true. But that's not the way it's supposed to be.

   Tell me this. When you go to Taco Bell, are you trying to show everyone how full you are?
   Huh?
   When you go to Goody's to pick up a new CD, do you take along all the CDs you already have and show off your collection?
   No, that's crazy.
   Well, why do you go to Goody's or 'cross the border'?
   Duh. To buy stuff.
   And why do you go to those places particularly?
   Because they have what I need.
   So why do you think most people go to church?
   Well, it's not for the tacos.
   Because they find something there that they need! They're not going to show everybody all the holiness they already have! They go because they need some holiness.
   And they get it at church?
   In a way, yes. In church we meet with God, and God has an effect on us. Now usually it's not all of a sudden—it takes time. So on Monday a lot of us are going to act just like people who don't know God. We struggle and stumble, but over time God changes us.

   You can spot a phony a light-year away, and so can your friends. In our churches, in our youth groups, we simply cannot pretend to be what we aren't. We need to be honest with people, honest with ourselves, and honest with God about who we really are: strugglers who sometimes mess up—big time—but strugglers who keep grabbing God's forgiveness and move on.

(continued on p. 51)

Isaiah had a vision of the Lord in the temple with a SWAT team of angels around him and smoke everywhere. *Holy, holy, holy is the Lord Almighty,* the angels sang. The Lord was definitely in the house.

How did Isaiah respond? *I am ruined!* he cried. He recognized how much junk he had in his own life. How could he stand before the holy Lord? *I am a man of unclean lips,* he confessed, *and I live among a people of unclean lips.*

In the vision, an angel took a hot coal from the altar and zapped Isaiah's lips with it. *Your guilt is taken away and your sin atoned for.* Then God gave Isaiah a job to do. (For more info, see Isaiah 6.)

The point here is not that you need to go around kissing barbecue grills. It's Jesus' blood that takes away our sin, not charcoal briquettes.

But when the Lord is in the house, we <u>have</u> <u>to</u> <u>be</u> real. We need to fess up to the sins that hold us back. No more pretending: the Lord burns away our masks.

Get real. Stop trying to impress God with how good you are, and just admit how much you need his power in your life.

Looking Back

Check the box if you have completed the assignment.

- ☐ I read chapter 4 in I Like Church, But...
- ☐ I completed Days 21–27.
- ☐ I prayed the Pierced Ears Prayer.
- ☐ I wrote down good things about my youth group or church.
- ☐ I raved to a friend about my youth group or church.
- ☐ I invited someone to youth group or church.
- ☐ I got together with two people outside my circle.
- ☐ I helped bring out a friend's potential.
- ☐ I read pages 50–51 (People Are Real).

moving forward

Theme 5:

When Jesus is in the house, it's a place where people are real.

Assignments for This Week:

- Read chapter 5 in I Like Church, But...
- Rave to a friend about your youth group or church (Action Step 2, p. 8).

Daily Assignments:

- Read the assigned Scripture passages and answer the questions in the journal.
- Pray the Pierced Ears Prayer (Action Step 1, pp. 6–7).
- Write down something good about your youth group or church on page 41 (Action Step 2, p. 8).

Before the End:

- Invite someone to youth group or church (Action Step 2, p. 8).
- Get together with two people outside your normal circle of friends (Action Step 3, p. 9).
- Help bring out a friend's potential (Action Step 4, p. 11).
- Take out the trash in your life (Action Step 5, p. 12).

theme 5
People Are Real

Read Acts 5:1-11; 20:32-37.

From: IamMiriam
To: An&Sapph

sapphy, I've been rethinking the advice I gave you—i do **NOT** think it's a good idea to lie. i think you'd better tell the truth. as rabbi abe says—honesty is the best policy. i must say i'm a bit concerned because you haven't answered my email and it's been a few days :-(are you just vacationing on the money you got from that land sale?????

:-e your sis, Miriam

KEYWORD

Covet—Coveting is getting distracted by what God has entrusted to someone else; it's wanting to be like someone you're not; it's questioning God's wisdom.

1. What did Ananias and Sapphira do wrong?

☐ They didn't give all their money.
☐ They wore stripes with plaid.
☐ They had funny names.
☐ They didn't like the apostles' shoes.
☐ They lied to the church and to God.
☐ They liked Jerry Lewis.
☐ They weren't spiritual enough.
☐ Other [   ]

2. In contrast, what examples does Paul give of his own integrity (Acts 20)?

3. We can learn many things about money, work, and integrity from these two passages. Which of these lessons is something that you need to pay special attention to?

	A lot	Some	A little
I shouldn't be envious of what other people have.	☐	☐	☐
I shouldn't expect handouts from others.	☐	☐	☐
It is more blessed to give than to receive.	☐	☐	☐
I should use what I have to help others.	☐	☐	☐
God is the source of integrity, not me.	☐	☐	☐
I shouldn't pretend to be more generous than I am.	☐	☐	☐
I shouldn't read Acts any more because it hits too close to home.	☐	☐	☐

unanswered Questions

Read Mark 11:15-17.

This is how Jesus began his last week on earth. After entering the city of Jerusalem like a king (Mark 11:1–11) he goes to the temple and throws his weight around like he owns the place.

WHOIS

Money Changers—Money changers had a real racket going. They sold 'official' sacrificial animals at terribly high prices. It's not that they were selling—it's that they were cheating. It's like one of those amusement parks where you have to pay $10 for a Coke.

1. Jesus made a comparison. He said the temple should be a house of prayer, but it had become a den of robbers. Describe the activities that might go on in each of these places.

House of prayer | **Den of robbers**

2. In what ways is your life like a den of robbers?
- ☐ Cheating
- ☐ Friendships on my terms
- ☐ Talking trash
- ☐ Other _____
- ☐ Taking advantage of people
- ☐ Lying when it suits me
- ☐ Not treating my body as a temple

3. In what ways is your life like a house of prayer?
- ☐ Strong relationship with Christ
- ☐ Looking for ways to help others
- ☐ Other _____
- ☐ Talking to God
- ☐ Telling people how good God is

4. If Christ were to throw out the trash in your life as he did in the temple, where would he start?

unanswered Questions

Read Psalm 15.

KEYWORD

<u>Usury</u>—Charging interest rates so high that people have trouble getting out of debt. Legal or illegal, usury is like loan-sharking.

1. Rephrase, in your own words, the questions in verse 1.

Bad news: The answer to verse 1 is no one. Good news: The answer also is anyone. We can't be holy on our own, but Christ takes care of it for us. (See Romans 3:22–24.)

2. The psalmist presents a list of virtues. How do you stack up against them? On the graph below, draw and shade bars to the levels that fit your life.

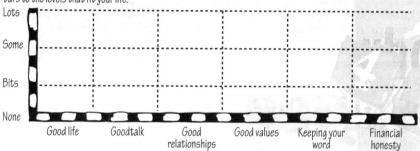

3. Whom do you know who scores high in each of these areas?

- Good life:
- Good talk:
- Good relationships:
- Good values:
- Keeping their word:
- Financial honesty:

4. According to the bar graph, which of these areas needs the most work in your life?

5. Ask the Lord what you can do to start improving in this area. In the space below, write any ideas he gives you.

unanswered Questions

Read Genesis 35:1-5.

KEYWORDS

Earrings—People in that neck of the woods, at that moment in history, carried their wealth in their ears and noses and around their wrists and ankles. We're not talking cheap hoops here; we're talking solid, serious gold.

Clothes—Some things never change: People get dressed up for special occasions, like, say, being rescued by God.

1. What did Jacob's household get rid of, and what did they do with those things?

2. Why did Jacob feel it was important to get rid of those things?

3. Jacob and his family were renewing a relationship with God. To do so they needed to reject the false gods they had been worshiping—they needed a fresh start. What false gods are still around in your life? (Are there things, people, or dreams that are more important to you than God and that might lead you away from him?)

What's the 411
Whatever you can't stop thinking about—that's your God.

4. How can you make a fresh start before the real God?

5. What effect did Jacob's family have on surrounding people after they took out the trash?

6. What effect would a church that took out the trash have on its community? Be specific.

unanswered questions

day 33
thursday, date

theme 5
People Are Real

Read Ephesians 4:22-32.

 Paul says we should put off the old self and put on the new. The rest of the passage describes what he means.

1. How much can you find in this passage for each category?

What should we put off?	What should we put on?

2. Why should we do these things?

3. Choose one thing from the list that you need to put off.

4. What can you do before your next meal to start the process of putting off whatever you have chosen? How could you get some help?

5. Now choose one thing from the list that you need to put on.

6. What can you do during the next 24 hours to start the process of putting on that thing? How could you get some help?

unanswered Questions

Read 1 Samuel 7:2–13.

KEYWORDS
<u>Baals and Ashtoreths</u>—Gods worshiped by the Canaanites; people often kept small images of these gods.

1. If this story were being made into a major motion picture, what would the advertisement look like?

2. In verse 3 Samuel gives a condition, a challenge, and a promise. What are they?
Condition:
Challenge:
Promise:

3. Later in the passage the enemies of God's people showed up. What did Samuel recommend the people do about this (verse 8)?

4. How did the Lord help the Israelites?

5. What enemies are you facing these days (spiritual, social, or physical)?

6. Are there things that you need to abandon? Do you need to call out to the Lord without stopping? How can you do this? What is the first step?

Unanswered Questions

theme 6.
We Make a Difference

I have 94 channels on my TV, but there's nothing good on. It's all stupid. Movies are stupid and getting stupider all the time. I mean, how much stuff can you blow up in two hours? Music is stupid, too. All the good bands are selling out. I can chat on the Internet with some guy in Luxembourg, but that's stupid, too. So I'll just sit here in the coffee shop complaining, if that's all right with you.

The point is, there is no point.

If you have that attitude, or something close to it, you're half right. There is a lot of stupid stuff going on in our world, a lot of pointless activity. If you set your sights on being Miss America, the NBA MVP, president of The United States, the next Bill Gates, or host of MTV's next dating game, you will probably be disappointed <u>even if</u> you accomplish your goal. You could reach that pinnacle and still not make much of a difference.

Does that mean <u>everything</u> is pointless? No. You can make a difference right now, today—maybe you're already doing so. As a Christian, you are already trafficking in the most valuable currency there is—the smiles of God. Empowered by God and aided by your church or youth group, you can make a difference in this world by doing God's business.

And what is God's business?

First of all, God wants us to <u>introduce people to him.</u> God is crazy about the human beings he created, and he wants to know us personally. Creation is a huge Hallmark card saying, *I love you all madly,* and the sacrificial death of Jesus was his *indescribable gift* (2 Corinthians 9:15). But people still need to accept God's love in order to get a strong relationship started. Through their words and actions, Christians can become matchmakers for God.

God also wants us to <u>help the needy.</u> This message is blasted throughout the pages of Scripture. God's people should be helping the hungry, the homeless, the imprisoned, the foreigners. While your classmates are busy watching stupid shows on Fox, you could be building a support network for the needy, getting your friends together to tutor slow learners, or volunteering in a city soup kitchen.

And God also wants us to <u>care for his creation.</u> The whole world is our responsibility. What does that mean? Taking care of the environment, doing what we can to not waste our resources—you know what we're talking about.

As we put our different skills together, encourage each other, and rely on the power of God, we can truly change the world. We change the world by changing individuals. We change individuals by helping with their physical needs, but especially by introducing them to Jesus. We introduce people to Jesus by giving them information, but especially by showing them Jesus' love.

Jesus said that we Christians are the *light of the world* and that we should let our light shine before other people so that *they may see your good deeds and praise your Father in heaven* (Matthew 5:14–16). When Jesus Christ is in the house, we leave the house with a mission—to shine the light of Christ throughout the world.

Looking Back

Check the box if you have completed the assignment.

- ☐ I read chapter 5 in I Like Church, But...
- ☐ I completed Days 28–34.
- ☐ I prayed the Pierced Ears Prayer.
- ☐ I wrote down good things about my youth group or church.
- ☐ I raved to a friend about my youth group or church.
- ☐ I invited someone to youth group or church.
- ☐ I got together with two people outside my circle.
- ☐ I helped bring out a friend's potential.
- ☐ I took out some trash from my life.
- ☐ I read page 59 (We Make a Difference).

moving forward

Theme 6:

When Jesus is in the house, it's a place where we make a difference.

Assignments for This Week:

- • Read chapter 6 in I Like Church, But...
- • Rave to a friend about your youth group or church (Action Step 2, p. 8).

Daily Assignments:

- • Read the assigned Scripture passages and answer the questions in the journal.
- • Pray the Pierced Ears Prayer (Action Step 1, pp. 6–7).
- • Write down something good about your youth group or church on page 41 (Action Step 2, p. 8).

Before the End:

- • Invite someone to youth group or church (Action Step 2, p. 8).
- • Get together with two people outside your normal circle of friends (Action Step 3, p. 9).
- • Help bring out a friend's potential (Action Step 4, p. 11).
- • Take out the trash in your life (Action Step 5, p. 12).

theme 6
We Make a
Difference

Read Acts 16:6-15.

To: SaulPaul
From: [encrypted]
come over to macedonia and help us!!!

We've talked about listening to people and dealing with their needs.
Now we're talking about making a difference—and not just with
people you come in contact with all the time.

WHOIS

<u>Worshiper of God</u>—The Bible suggests that when people sincerely worship
God as they understand him, God reveals himself to them more clearly.

1. How did God call Paul and his companions into Macedonia?

2. Is there anything in your life that seems discouraging (a closing door) that may turn out to be God leading you in another direction (an opening door)?

3. Has there been a time when God disrupted your plans in order to get you to do something else?

4. What might God's plans be for you? How could he be asking you to make a difference?

5. This was groundbreaking stuff Paul was doing. Is there something groundbreaking that you can do for the spread of the gospel? Consider spreading the Good News to:
- [ ] The Internet.
- [ ] Gang members.
- [ ] Deaf people.
- [ ] Prisoners.
- [ ] A faraway land.
- [ ] People unable to read
- [ ] Native Americans.
- [ ] Foreign students.

unanswered questions

theme 6
We Make a
Difference

day 37
monday,
date

Read Matthew 25:31-40.

1. How does this passage make you feel?

2. How does Christ feel when we take care of the needs of people?

3. How does Christ feel when we ignore the needs of people?

4. Where might you help a stranger or someone needing clothes or a sick person or a person in prison?

5. Have you seen . . .

	Yes	No
• A stranger who wasn't from out of town?		
• Someone thirsty who didn't need water?		
• Someone hungry for something besides food?		
• Someone naked but still wearing clothes?		

6. Can you think of two people you know in each of these categories?
• Stranger:
• Thirsty person:
• Hungry person :
• Naked person:

Unanswered Questions

day 38
tuesday,
date

Read Genesis 1:28–31.

Let's start from the very beginning, at the point when God put people on the earth—male and female, created in his image—and said, *"It's all yours. Go have some fun!"*

1. What did God command?

2. After God finished his creation, what did he think of what he had made?

3. What responsibility came when Adam and Eve were chosen to rule the creation? (See Genesis 2:15.) What else did God ask Adam and Eve to do in the garden?

4. We know that the people of the earth are broken by sin. But the earth itself is broken also (Romans 8:18–25). In what ways do you notice this brokenness?

5. As Christians we have a mission to serve the broken world. Do you think we also have a calling to repair the earth however we can? If so, give some examples of what might be done.

6. What can you do to make a difference?

unanswered Questions

theme 6
We Make a
Difference

day 39
wednesday,
date

Read Luke 14:12-14.

 Jesus is at a party where everybody, including the host, is working hard to look good.

1. What's wrong with being paid back?

2. Suppose this passage were used as a basis for a new MTV series. Suggest some ideas for the format.
• Title:
• Characters:

• Situation:

• Other elements:

3. Sometimes if you want to make a difference you need to go beyond your usual routine. Where would you go to look for people who are poor, crippled, lame, or blind? How could you make a difference in their lives?

unanswered Questions

day 40
thursday,
date

Read Isaiah 58:6-11.

KEYWORD

Yoke—A harness used to join animals together. It symbolizes slavery.

1. Fasting was a ritual done as an attempt to please God. But how does God describe the kind of fast he prefers?

2. What promise follows the instructions that are given?

3. What do people in your community need to be set free from?

4. What people can you think of who are oppressed today?

5. What kinds of people today need to be shown compassion and justice?
- ☐ People with AIDS
- ☐ The homeless
- ☐ The poor
- ☐ People with disabilities
- ☐ Ethnic groups
- ☐ Other [   ]

6. What is an example of malicious talk you have heard, perhaps accompanied by a pointing finger?

7. What can your church or youth group do to provide food, clothing, or shelter to the poor, homeless, or hungry?

Unanswered Questions

theme 6
**We Make a
Difference**

day 41
friday,
date

Read James 2:14-17.

What's the 411

James isn't saying you earn your faith. He's just saying that genuine faith is accompanied by actions.

1. Write four lines of a rap or a poem about this passage.

2. Verses 14 and 16 contain questions. What are the answers?

3. If you were the brother or sister who needed food and clothing, how would you feel if someone gave you sympathetic words but didn't do anything?

4. In what specific ways do you need to put your faith into action?

unanswered Questions

The college choir was touring the Midwest, singing at various churches. After each concert, people from the churches would take choir members home and put them up for the night. One pleasant church member drove two young men from the choir to his home, let them off at the curb, and said, *Go right in and make yourselves at home. I just have to park the car.*

They did as the man said, letting themselves in and sitting politely on the couch. There they waited for the man to come in. And they waited. And waited.

They were in the wrong house.

I (Randy) have felt that way at some churches I've attended. *Go on in and sit down. God will be right with you.* But I wait and wait and God just doesn't show. Eventually I figure I'm in the wrong house.

Some churches are just so busy <u>doing</u> church that they never notice the Guest of Honor is absent. When God does try to make an appearance—when a church member starts speaking from the heart, or when a preacher delivers a strong challenge, or when a homeless person slips into the back pew—everyone seems a bit embarrassed.

In Jesus' day the religious leaders acted the same way. They were so busy conducting their religious activities that they ignored—and actually <u>opposed</u>—their own Messiah. Jesus rode into town on Palm Sunday, greeted by a cheering mob, and the leaders said, *Keep it down! Can't you see we're trying to be religious here?*

Ironically, their whole religion focused on getting ready for the Messiah. The Pharisees were fanatics about keeping the law (and making sure that everyone else did, too) <u>so that the Messiah would come.</u> Well, here he was on their doorstep, and they were complaining about the noise.

Opening night of <u>Carousel</u>, the show I directed last year, I was scurrying around, fixing last-minute problems. I needed to talk to the lighting crew, but a couple of student ushers almost didn't let me in. They didn't know me; I didn't have a ticket.

Jesus probably feels the same way at some churches. *Hey, I'm <u>directing</u> this show! If I'm not there, <u>there is no show</u>. Let me in!*

But he is denied admission. *Sorry, bud. I don't care if you're the Prince of Wales, you need a ticket. Nice sandals, though.*

If your church is like this, what can you do? Smuggle Jesus in. Remind your church that Jesus Christ is (or should be) at the center of what you do. On the first Palm Sunday, children were singing praises. If kids can do it, certainly you can.

But some youth groups have a problem. They're all about having fun and not about meeting with Jesus. Don't get me wrong. Jesus can have fun with the best of us. But we must be serious about meeting with him.

When Jesus Christ is in the house, we know that we're in the presence of the living God. He is the life of the party, the director of the show. He is why we're there.

Looking Back

Check the box if you have completed the assignment.

☐ I read chapter 6 in I Like Church, But...
☐ I completed Days 35–41.
☐ I prayed the Pierced Ears Prayer.
☐ I wrote down good things about my youth group or church.
☐ I raved to a friend about my youth group or church.
☐ I invited someone to youth group or church.
☐ I got together with two people outside my circle.
☐ I helped bring out a friend's potential.
☐ I took out some trash from my life.
☐ I read page 67 (God Shows Up).

moving forward

Theme 7:

When Jesus is in the house, it's a place where God shows up.

Theme 8:

When Jesus is in the house, it's a place where the future looks bright.

Assignments for This Week:

• Read chapters 7 and 8 in I Like Church, But...
• Rave to a friend about your youth group or church (Action Step 2, p. 8).
• Read page 73 (The Future Looks Bright).

Daily Assignments:

• Read the assigned Scripture passages and answer the questions in the journal.
• Pray the Pierced Ears Prayer (Action Step 1, pp. 6–7).
• Write down something good about your youth group or church on page 41 (Action Step 2, p. 8).

Before the End:

• Invite someone to youth group or church (Action Step 2, p. 8).
• Get together with two people outside your normal circle of friends (Action Step 3, p. 9).
• Help bring out a friend's potential (Action Step 4, p. 11).
• Take out the trash in your life (Action Step 5, p. 12).

theme 7
God Shows Up

Read Acts 4:23-31.

From: WEATHERNET
To: Weather.listserv
REPORT FROM THE JUDEAN WEATHER COUNCIL
The earthquake last Sunday measured 3.2 on the ben-Richter scale. Its epicenter has been traced to a house in Jerusalem where a group of people were holding some kind of religious service. No injuries have been reported.

What's the 411

Peter and John were thrown in jail for preaching about Jesus and released with a stern warning.

1. What did the believers ask for?

2. How did God make his presence known?

3. How would you feel if your youth group's or church's prayer was followed by an earthquake?
- [ ] Nauseous
- [ ] Shaken but not stirred
- [ ] Scared
- [ ] Other [_____]

4. How does God make his presence known in your church?

5. How does God make his presence known in your life?

6. What happened when God showed up with Peter and John?

7. What happens when God shows up in your life or church?

unanswered Questions

Read Mark 11:1-10.

1. What was the crowd's response to Jesus?

2. What were the people expecting from Jesus (verse 10)?

3. What do you think these people would say if you were to travel back through time and tell them that five days later Jesus would be crucified?

4. What has been the most triumphant day of your life during the last three years?
- ☐ Acing a test
- ☐ Winning a championship
- ☐ Landing a date with someone special
- ☐ Performing in a successful show
- ☐ Getting your driver's license
- ☐ Winning a trophy
- ☐ Your birthday or another celebration
- ☐ Other _____

5. It's easy to pray to a God of triumph, but harder to praise a God who allows suffering. How can we worship God more completely?

6. What happened when God showed up on the first Palm Sunday?

7. At what time in your life did God show up in a significant way? Was anything surprising to you? What was your reaction?

Unanswered Questions

Read Psalm 84.

1. If you were to set this psalm to music, what style of music would work best?

2. How would you describe the psalmist's attitude?

3. When God shows up in his dwelling place, what happens?

4. What happens in the house? (Note verse 4.)

5. Indicate how much you've felt the presence of God on different days of the previous week.

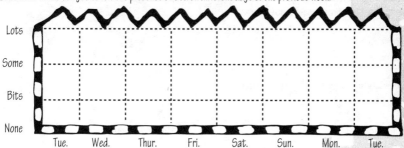

Lots
Some
Bits
None

Tue. Wed. Thur. Fri. Sat. Sun. Mon. Tue.

6. Circle the one or two high points. Why were they so high?

7. Circle the one or two low points. Why were they so low?

unanswered Questions

theme 1
God Shows Up

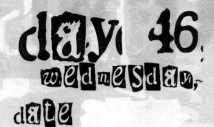
day 46
wednesday,
date

Read 1 Timothy 3:14-16.

1. When God showed up as a man (Jesus) on the earth, what happened?

2. How does this passage define God's household?

3. Whose family is the church?

4. When you don't know how to conduct yourself in the house, where can you look for instructions?

5. Have you discovered anything in the past 46 days that will help you know how to conduct yourself in the house? What are the top three things you have learned?

1.

2.

3.

6. How do you know God is living in your church?

7. How alive is your church? (Use a scale of 1 to 10; 1=Corpse, 10=Olympic athlete.)

1   5   10

8. If outsiders looked at your church, how alive would they think God is?

❑ Comatose
❑ Ready for the marathon
❑ Dead
❑ Just thinking
❑ Alive and kicking
❑ Other [   ]

unanswered questions

theme 1
The Future Looks Bright

What are you going to do when you graduate?

I (Randy) always ask that of the high school seniors I know, and I get lots of different answers. Some know exactly what college they're entering and what they'll major in. Some are joining the armed forces or jumping right into a job-training program. Others seem aimless.

Aimlessness seems to be growing.

If you believe the magazines, it's the epidemic of the new generation. You will never make as much money as your parents, so you'll probably be living with them until you're 43. Even if you do make money, the national debt is going to be so high that dollars will be worthless. Terrorists will probably blow up Washington, but hey, that's probably a good thing. Unless, of course, we're talking about Seattle.

(Are you as sick of that *Gen X* stuff as I am?)

What does <u>your</u> future look like? Good? Bad? Ugly? Is it so bright you have to wear shades?

There are always questions. Even seniors who have a course of study mapped out through grad school will probably change majors five times. You grow, and your future grows with you.

Things may look bleak for you now, but who knows what surprises lie ahead? My friend Luke was one of those aimless ones, planning to get a minimum wage job and grab a few courses at the community college. With help from myself and others, he developed his acting talent and is now headed for a prestigious arts school. You never know what may happen. That is both exciting and scary.

As Christians, though, we have a special assurance that will get us through the scary times. We don't know what the future holds, <u>but we know who holds the future.</u> With his resurrection, Jesus Christ proved that he is ultimately in control of the future—he even has power over death. *Who shall separate us from the love of Christ?* cheers the apostle Paul. *Shall trouble or hardship or . . . danger?* (Romans 8:35).

Nope.

We may still have to go through undesirable circumstances, but we know that Christ goes with us and that we'll end up in eternity with him.

You probably don't spend a whole lot of time thinking about eternity, and that's understandable. But eternity casts its shadow on every day of our lives. We make decisions based on what we expect to happen in the future. If people have no hope, they develop an attitude of *Eat, drink, and be merry, for tomorrow we die.* Their daily decisions about relationships, sex, work, money, drugs, alcohol, fitness, or the environment are based on their here-and-now hopelessness.

But we are not like those who have no hope. We try to honor Christ with our decision, because we know he's the one who holds our future in his hands.

In college, I heard a speaker talk about *you young people who are preparing for life.* <u>Preparing for life?</u> I thought we were already living!

Your future is now. Live in the light of the living Christ. When Jesus Christ is in the house, his people celebrate. He has conquered death once and for all, and he promises us an eternal life full of joy and power.

theme 8
The Future Looks Bright

day 47
thursday, date

Read Matthew 16:13-21.

1. So you're out playing *midnight basketball* with Jesus and the gang when he adds this question to the mix: *Who do you say I am?* As you think about your classmates and friends, how do you answer?

2. *But who do you say I am?* he asks. Now how do you respond?

3. According to today's Bible passage, what is the church built on? What does this mean?

4. Jesus said the *gates of Hades* wouldn't overcome the church. Obviously he was talking about the power of evil, but where do you see this power attacking the church today?

5. We've been talking about the future, and sometimes when we hear God's promises, the future looks so bright we have to wear sunscreen. (Or something like that.) But put yourself back in today's scripture. As you're listening to Jesus in verses 17–19, how bright does the future look?

Verses 17–19
SPF Factor 1 _____ SPF Factor 90
(Dismal)   (Dazzling)

Now as you read verse 21, how bright does the future look?

Verse 21
SPF Factor 1 _____ SPF Factor 90
(Dismal)   (Dazzling)

6. Jesus asked Peter, *Who do you say I am?* and then he told Peter who <u>Peter</u> was. Who does Jesus say you are?

unanswered Questions

Read Psalm 22.

1. This is a very picturesque psalm. Choose a verse or two and draw a picture of what the passage is talking about.

2. How does the first half of this psalm (verses 1–21) make you feel?

3. How does the last half of the psalm (verses 22–31) make you feel?

4. Jot down the specific words that led to your feelings.

First half	Second half

5. Some parts of this psalm seem to predict Jesus' experience on the cross. Which verses would you say are prophetic?

6. How can you declare his name (verse 22) in your church (or youth group) and outside of it?

unanswered Questions

theme 8
The Future Looks Bright

day 49
Saturday,
date

Read 1 Peter 1:3-9.

1. Why does Peter want to praise God?

2. When he says we have a *living hope*, what does he mean?
- [ ] The belief that we'll go to heaven when we die.
- [ ] A meaningful life on earth.
- [ ] We hope we can go on living, rather than dying in some terrible chariot crash.
- [ ] Other [   ]

3. What *trials* have you had to face recently?

4. What does this passage tell you about these trials?

5. According to this passage and others you've read in this Adventure, describe a proper attitude for those who are *in the house*—that is, Christians.

unanswered Questions

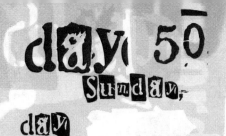

day 50
Sunday, day

Read Acts 9:1-19.

From: SaulPaul
To: HiPriest
i quit—will explain later.

1. Make-overs are all the rage these days. You can't turn on a talk show without someone crowing about the self-esteem that comes from a new 'do. Anyway, Saul (later known as Paul) got a make-over of his own after he had a vision of the risen Christ. Describe the changes.

Before		After
Looks		
Skills		
Attitude		
Goal in life		

 By the way, this isn't the same Ananias you read about on Day 28/29. That guy is still dead.

2. How did Ananias react to what God was doing?

3. In what way have you *encountered* the risen Christ? Briefly describe how you met Jesus.

4. How has that encounter changed you?

5. What *mission* can you accept to share what Christ has done for you?

6. As you complete your Adventure today, what is the most important thing you want to remember as you move ahead with your life?

Unanswered Questions

Looking Back

Check the box if you have completed the assignment.
- ☐ I read chapters 1–8 in I Like Church, But…
- ☐ I completed Days 1–50.
- ☐ I prayed the Pierced Ears Prayer.
- ☐ I wrote down good things about my youth group or church.
- ☐ I raved to friends about my youth group or church.
- ☐ I invited someone to youth group or church.
- ☐ I got together with two people outside my circle.
- ☐ I helped bring out a friend's potential.
- ☐ I took out some trash from my life.

What are the most important things you learned during this adventure?

Unanswered Questions

Tell us your story.

We've been praying that this Adventure would make a difference in your life. And we would love to hear your story. As you're finishing up this Adventure, we're already hard at work on a new one. But the Adventure is for you. So send us your comments and feedback. We'd love to hear from you.

Randy   Jon   Mitch

The Chapel Ministries
Editorial Department
Box 30
Wheaton, IL 60189

Or send an email with your comments to: T50DSA@aol.com

YOU FINISHED THE ADVENTURE—NOW WHAT?

Daily Scripture reading and prayer have been a part of your life for the past 50 days. But while the Adventure ends after 50 days, the habits you formed don't need to. Consider these options to keep going down the path this Adventure started you on.

• The *I'm So Confused* 50-Day Spiritual Adventure
I'm So Confused!
Following Christ When Life Gets Crazy

Student Journal by Randy Petersen $6.00
When Life Become a Maze Guidebook by David Mains $6.00

• Scripture Union Devotionals

Scripture Union subscriptions are for a whole year! There are devotionals for young people of all ages. One to One is for youth ages 11–14, and Discovery is a personal application guide for mature young people and adults.

✂ --

ORDER FORM
I'm So Confused 50-Day Spiritual Adventure

	Price	Qty	Total
☐ Student Journal	$6.00	_____	_____
☐ When Life Becomes a Maze Guidebook	$6.00	_____	_____
	Subtotal		_____

Add 10% for UPS shipping/handling ($4.00 minimum)   _____ _____
Canadian or Illinois residents add 7% GST/sales tax

	TOTAL		_____

Scripture Union Guides
All devotionals will be sent every three months for one year (tax and shipping included).
• Yes! I would like an annual subscription to:

	Price	Qty	Total
☐ Discovery	$20.00	_____	_____
☐ One to One	$20.00	_____	_____
	TOTAL		_____

TOTAL AMOUNT ENCLOSED _____

Please fill out the information below:

Your name _____

Address _____

State/Prov _____ Zip/Code _____ Phone _____

I'd like to pay by: ☐ Check ☐ Money Order ☐ VISA ☐ MasterCard ☐ Discover

Make checks payable to: The Chapel Ministries
      Send this order form to:
      The Chapel Ministries, Box 30, Wheaton, IL 60189
      or call 1-800-224-2735 (in Canada 1-800-461-4114) for credit card orders

SUG497